# PACK IT UP

## Surface Area and Volume

**Chloe Lane**

## Consultants

**Pamela Dase, M.A.Ed.**
National Board Certified Teacher

**Barbara Talley, M.S.**
Texas A&M University

## Publishing Credits

Dona Herweck Rice, *Editor-in-Chief*
Robin Erickson, *Production Director*
Lee Aucoin, *Creative Director*
Timothy J. Bradley, *Illustration Manager*
Sara Johnson, M.S.Ed., *Senior Editor*
Aubrie Nielsen, M.S.Ed., *Associate Education Editor*
Jennifer Kim, M.A.Ed., *Associate Education Editor*
Neri Garcia, *Senior Designer*
Stephanie Reid, *Photo Editor*
Rachelle Cracchiolo, M.S.Ed., *Publisher*

## Image Credits

## Teacher Created Materials

5301 Oceanus Drive
Huntington Beach, CA 92649-1030
http://www.tcmpub.com

**ISBN 978-1-4333-3461-0**

© 2012 Teacher Created Materials, Inc.

# TABLE OF CONTENTS

# A FRESH START

I am moving into a new house today! Things have been busy around here. My whole family has been packing up our house to get ready to move to a new town. The moving truck is arriving this morning to load up our stuff.

Moving makes me feel a little bit nervous and **anxious** (ANGK-shuhs). First, I have to change schools and make new friends. Meeting new people can be really hard sometimes. Second, I have to get all my stuff organized and packed, and then unpacked and organized again. That's a lot of work, but I'm also very excited because our new house is really cool!

Shipping boxes come in different shapes. Some are in the shape of a **cube**. Some are **rectangular prisms**. When people move, all shapes and sizes of boxes are needed. The boxes help organize a family's belongings. Boxes also protect items as they are moved from one place to another.

The first thing my family did when we started packing was to gather all different kinds of boxes. Our boxes had to **vary** in size because we needed different sizes to hold different objects.

We started by packing one room at a time. We sorted items so they would fit correctly in a box. Small things were often packed together. For example, cups and plates went into a small box. Larger objects sometimes needed a whole box all to themselves. Some large items we packed were our television and computer monitor.

## What Is Volume?

**Volume** is the amount of space occupied by a **three-dimensional** (dih-MEN-shuhn-uhl) object. Volume determines the number of cubes of a certain size that will fill a three-dimensional space. It is measured in cubic units.

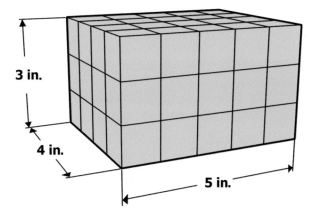

The volume of this box is 60 in.³ The "in.³" stands for cubic inches. That means 60 1-inch cubes would fill the box.

The very important final step in packing each box was to label it. We wanted to make sure that our boxes were carried to the right room. We did not want our bathroom items unloaded in the kitchen of our new home!

## LET'S EXPLORE MATH

Most packing boxes are rectangular prisms. So are many other containers, such as the terrarium below. To find the volume of a rectangular prism, use the **formula** $V = lwh$. The formula tells you to multiply the length ($l$) by the width ($w$) by the height ($h$).

**a.** Use the formula for the volume of a rectangular prism to find the volume of a terrarium that is 21 in. long, 13 in. wide, and 14 in. high.

**b.** What would be the height of a terrarium that is 3 ft. long and 1 ft. wide if the volume is 6 ft.$^3$

# DOING MY PART

My family had a lot to pack, so we all pitched in to help. I was in charge of packing my own room. My parents figured that I would know how to sort my own belongings into boxes. Plus, in the new house, I'll want to unpack my stuff and set up my new room.

## Safe Packing

When you pack a box, you want to make sure that delicate items will not break. One way to do that is to wrap items carefully in newspaper or bubble wrap. Some people also might include foam packing peanuts to help cushion items inside the box so they do not knock against each other.

My brother helped me decide which size boxes to use.

My room is my own private space that I like to have a certain way.

I had to sort through my things because I have stuff that fit in small, medium, and large boxes. My soccer cleats and shin guards were packed in a small box. Most of my sweatshirts fit in a medium-sized box. I used a large box for my computer and my speakers.

Some of my most prized possessions (puh-ZESH-uhnz) are my books. I have a bookshelf full of them! Believe it or not, I still have books that were given to me when I first started school.

Books are heavy, so when you pack them you have to use small boxes. If you don't, you might not be able to pick up the box.

LET'S EXPLORE MATH

Look at this shipping box.

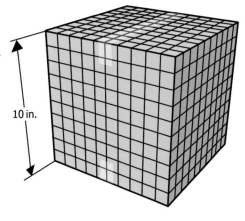

10 in.

a. How can you find the number of cubes in the layer at the top of the box?

b. How many of these layers are there in the whole box?

c. Find the volume of this shipping box. Remember to label your answer correctly.

d. Explain why you can also use the volume formula for a rectangular prism to find the volume of a cube.

# WAYS TO MOVE

People can move across the street or across the world. They move into new homes or new apartments, but the way they move may be different. Some people move themselves. They ask family or friends to lend a hand and help pack boxes and load a car or truck. They may even rent a moving truck so they can move more things in fewer trips. People who move themselves might not have as much stuff to move, so they can handle it on their own. By moving themselves, they will save some money, too.

People in different parts of the world move in different ways. This family uses a boat to move across Lake Malawi in Malawi, Africa.

The nomadic Kochis of Afghanistan move from northern areas to south and southeast Afghanistan in camel caravans. They seek warmer climates and good pastures for their animals.

People can move some of their own things in their car. Look at the approximate dimensions of the trunk of this car.

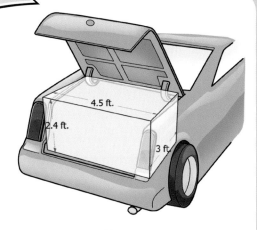

4.5 ft.

2.4 ft.

3 ft.

Now look at the space in the back of a moving truck.

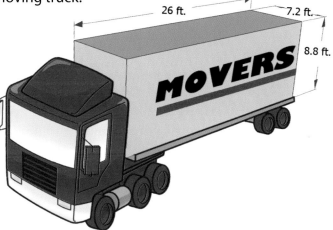

26 ft.

7.2 ft.

8.8 ft.

MOVERS

**a.** What are the volumes of these two different spaces?

**b.** About how many loads from the trunk of the car would fit into the moving truck? Round your answer to the nearest ten.

Many people hire professional movers to help them move to a new place. They hire people to load boxes and furniture into a large moving truck. Then, after they arrive at their new home, the movers arrive with the truck and unload it. The movers try to make sure that all the boxes go into the correct rooms. This is why labeling the boxes is so **essential** (uh-SEN-shuhl)!

# HIRING MOVERS

My family decided to hire movers because we have so much stuff, and our furniture is very heavy. My parents thought that having movers help us would make the whole day go much smoother. I think they were right!

The movers have a huge job to do in a short amount of time. Of course, they have to be strong enough to carry heavy things. They also have to be careful not to break anything.

Our movers wrapped our couch in plastic to protect it during the move.

## Watch Out for the Fragile Box!

Many people who move decide to label certain boxes as "fragile." This means that the contents of the box are easily breakable. When movers see a "fragile" label, they know to take special care with the box.

Another important part of a mover's job is to load the truck carefully. Movers have to place the boxes in the truck in a special way. They usually put heavy boxes on the bottom and stack lighter boxes on top. They also have to make sure that boxes are arranged so they will not shift around when the truck is moving.

Our movers did a great job. They loaded the truck and drove all of our stuff to our new house. We followed behind them in our own car. When they first arrived, my mom gave them a tour of our new house and showed them where the kitchen, living room, bathrooms, and bedrooms were. She reminded them to put each box in the right room. All they had to do was read the labels to know where everything was supposed to go.

After a long lunch break, it was time for everybody to get back to work. As the movers unloaded the truck, we had to start unpacking boxes. My dad started in the kitchen. He unpacked a lot of our dishes and cookware. Because the kitchen items had been neatly sorted before they were packed, it was easy for him to unpack and put everything away.

## Moving Equipment

Movers use different equipment to help them move large and heavy pieces of furniture. They might use a dolly, which is a cart with wheels that people use to help move heavy objects. A dolly makes it much easier to load and unload boxes. They may also use blankets and straps to cover furniture and secure items inside the truck.

My dad unpacked boxes in the kitchen. He unpacked a small box filled mostly with cans of soup. Soup cans are shaped like a **cylinder**. The formula for the volume of a cylinder is $V = \pi r^2 h$. Find the **area** of the circular base ($\pi r^2$), and then multiply it by the height ($h$). The volume of a cylinder is measured in cubic units just like any other three-dimensional object. When you imagine it filled with cubes, though, some of those cubes will not be whole because of its rounded shape.

**Key**

$\pi$ = pi ≈ 3.14

$r$ = **radius**

$h$ = height

Area of a Circle

$A = \pi r^2$

Volume of a Cylinder

$V = \pi r^2 h$

3.5 cm

10 cm

Look at the soup can above. Use 3.14 for the value of $\pi$.

**a.** What is the area of the circular base? Round your answer to the nearest hundredth.

**b.** What is the volume of the can of soup?

**c.** What is the volume of a soup can with a radius of 4.2 cm and a height of 11 cm? Round your answer to the nearest hundredth.

# EXPLORING THE BACKYARD

While the movers worked to unload the boxes, I took a break to check out my new house. It is much bigger than our old house. My favorite part is our new backyard because we have a patio where we can hang out when the weather is warm. There is also a nice lawn, but the best part of all is the swimming pool and hot tub!

## Safety First

If you have a pool on your property, you should have a fence or wall around it. Some places actually have laws that require a pool to be enclosed. This allows you to lock out young kids or other people who cannot swim. Homeowners are responsible for the safety of the people around their pools.

I am really looking forward to using our pool this summer. I have never lived anywhere that had a pool before. I noticed that our pool is rectangular-shaped, and the hot tub is cylindrical. I realize that if I find their volumes, I can figure out how much water they both hold. Of course, the pool has stairs and the hot tub has seats, so my calculations (kal-kyuh-LEY-shuhnz) will not be exact.

LET'S EXPLORE MATH

Look at the drawings of my pool and hot tub. Use 3.14 for the value of π.

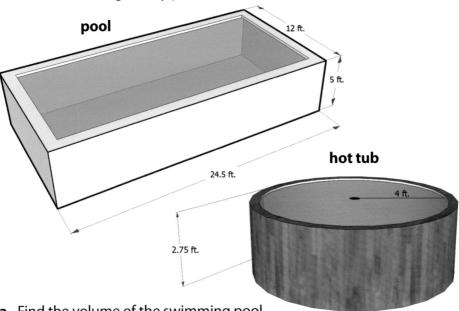

pool

12 ft.

5 ft.

24.5 ft.

2.75 ft.

hot tub

4 ft.

**a.** Find the volume of the swimming pool.

**b.** Find the volume of the hot tub. Round your answer to the nearest hundredth.

**c.** Given that the hot tub has seats, would the actual volume of the hot tub be greater or less than your answer for problem **b**?

**d.** Why is the formula for finding the volume of the pool different from the formula for finding the volume of the hot tub?

# A FRESH COAT OF PAINT

After exploring the backyard, I explore the house a bit more. I know that many of the rooms in our new house will need to be repainted, and my dad asked me to help. He wants me to paint all of the surfaces inside our garage—the floor, ceiling, walls, and garage door! I need to figure out how much paint to buy. The dimensions of the floor are 22 feet by 24 feet, and the height is 10 feet. Using these dimensions, I can find its **surface area**. This will help me figure out how much paint to buy.

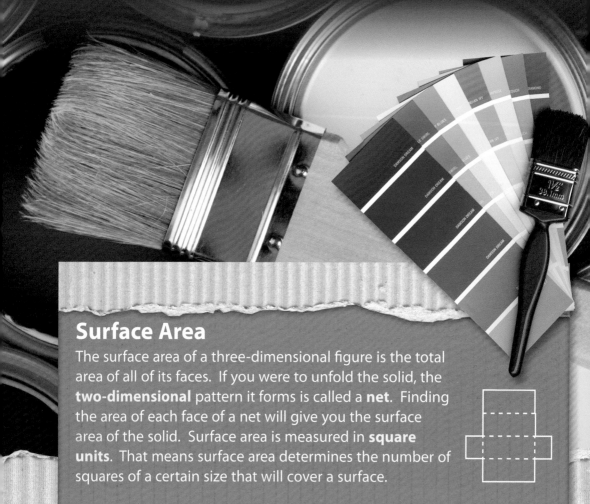

## Surface Area

The surface area of a three-dimensional figure is the total area of all of its faces. If you were to unfold the solid, the **two-dimensional** pattern it forms is called a **net**. Finding the area of each face of a net will give you the surface area of the solid. Surface area is measured in **square units**. That means surface area determines the number of squares of a certain size that will cover a surface.

Find the surface area of the garage.

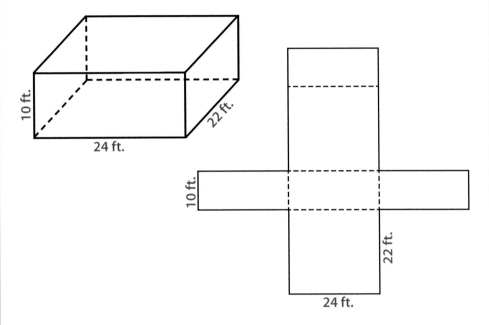

**a.** Start by finding the area of the garage floor. Then double that area to include the ceiling.

**b.** Find the area of one of the side walls. Then double that area to include the opposite wall with the same area.

**c.** Find the area of the back wall. Then double that area to include the front wall.

**d.** Add the areas of the six faces. What is the surface area? Be sure to label your answer in square feet (ft.$^2$).

**e.** My grandmother's garage measures 22 ft. by 20 ft. by 8 ft. How many cans of paint would it take to paint the interior of her garage if one can of paint will cover 388 ft.$^2$?

**f.** Use your work to write a formula for the surface area of a rectangular prism. (*Hint:* Use *l* for length, *w* for width, and *h* for height in your formula.)

# THE SHAPE OF MY ROOM

Time to get back to today's job—unpacking! I'm in charge of unpacking the boxes in my bedroom, and I also have to decide how to arrange the furniture in my room.

My new room is the shape of a rectangular prism. I have to figure out how to make space for all the furniture that I have, so I measure my new room to make sure I still have space for everything. I'm trying to figure out where to put my bed, nightstand, and dresser.

This is what my room will look like once it is painted and decorated.

Find the surface area of this bedroom in the new house. Be sure to include the floor, ceiling, and all four walls.

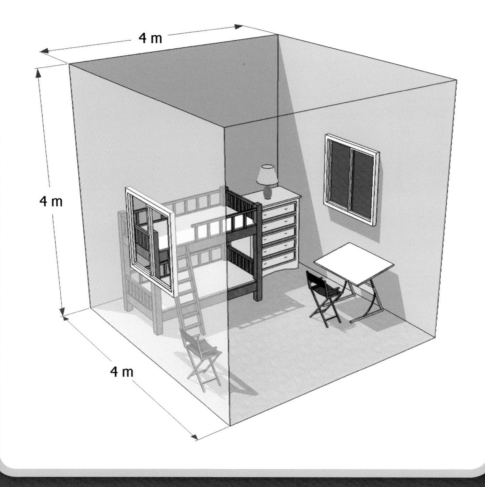

4 m

4 m

4 m

Once the furniture is all organized, I can start putting stuff away. I am already excited about sleeping in my new bedroom tonight.

# MOVING FURNITURE AROUND

Setting up a room and arranging furniture in the best possible way can be like solving a puzzle. You want the furniture in your bedroom to fit nicely and look nice, too. You also want space to move around and to hang out comfortably.

Along with my furniture, I need to find a spot for my new aquarium. My aquarium is a cylinder. I used to keep my fish in a bowl on my dresser, but the new aquarium is too large to sit on my dresser. I'll have to find a place for it on the floor.

Find the surface area of the cylindrical aquarium.

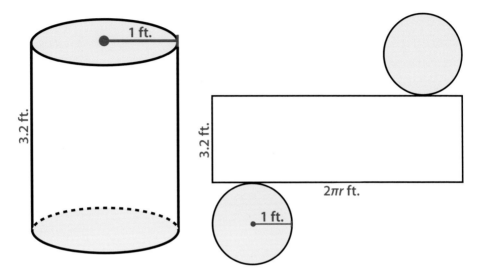

Find the area of the two circles and the rectangle, then add them together. Use 3.14 for the value of $\pi$.

**a.** Find the area of the rectangle. Notice that the length of the curved surface is equal to the **circumference** of the circle, $2\pi r$ or $\pi d$, where $r$ is the radius of the circle and $d$ is the **diameter**. Round to the nearest hundredth.

**b.** Find the area of one of the circles. (Remember that the area of a circle is found using the formula $A = \pi r^2$). Double that area to include both circles. Round your answer to the nearest hundredth.

**c.** Find the sum of the areas of the faces. Label your answer in square units.

**d.** Use your work to write a formula for the surface area of a cylinder.

# FILLING UP THE CLOSET

The last step of unpacking is to put all of my clothes away. I can put away a lot of my things in my dresser, but I have some clothes that I need to hang in the closet. In my old house, my closet was very small and not very **functional**. There wasn't much room for anything except hanging clothes. In my new house, I have a much bigger closet that I can use for both clothes and **storage**. I know from looking at other houses with my parents that closet space is an important feature of any living space.

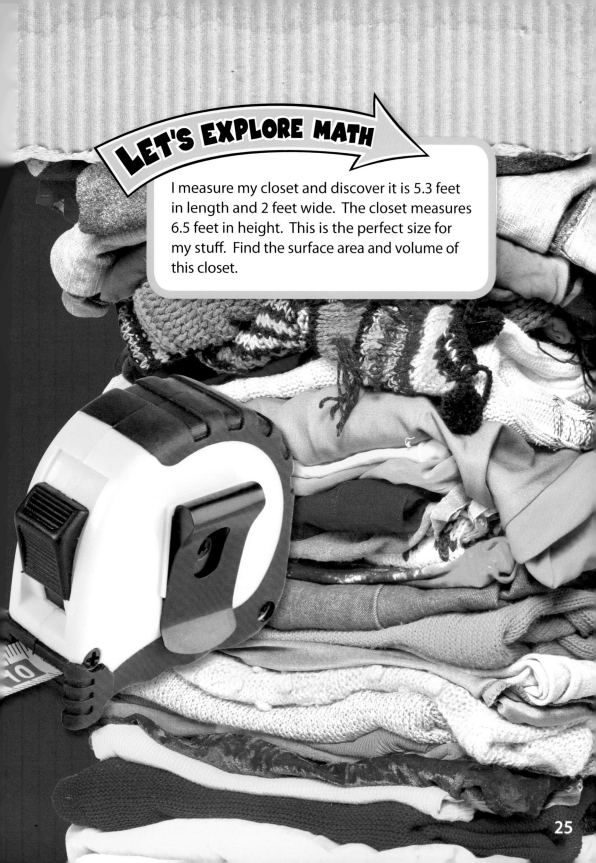

I measure my closet and discover it is 5.3 feet in length and 2 feet wide. The closet measures 6.5 feet in height. This is the perfect size for my stuff. Find the surface area and volume of this closet.

# THE END OF THE DAY

Wow, it's been a long day! I'm sore and tired and happy to be going to bed soon. My family worked hard today to move into our new home. We all had to pitch in and get the job done. Even though we still have a lot of boxes to unpack, we are definitely settled enough to feel comfortable in our new home.

I'm still feeling a bit nervous, especially about starting at a new school.  But I realized today that change is good. Moving into this new house feels like a fresh start.  I think it's going to be a wonderful place to live.

## Comparing Containers

Kayla is moving into a new home. She wants to choose a container to use to move a few of her personal items. She is comparing the dimensions of three containers.

- Container A is a rectangular prism. It is 5.3 feet long and 3.1 feet wide. It has a volume of 36.17 ft.$^3$

- Container B is a cube. It measures 4.4 feet on each side.

- Container C is a cylinder. Its height is 4.75 feet. It has a radius of 1.08 feet.

# Solve It!

**a.** Container B is a cube. What does that mean about the length, width, and height of the container? Find the volume of Container B. Round your answer to the nearest hundredth.

**b.** Find the volume of Container C in cubic feet. Round your answer to the nearest tenth.

**c.** Find the surface areas of each container in square feet.

**d.** If Kayla needs to know which container will take up the least amount of room in the moving truck, which measurement is most important? Why?

Use the steps below to help you solve the problems.

**Step 1:** Use the formula for the volume of a cube, $V = lwh$, to solve problem **a**.

**Step 2:** Use the formula for the volume of a cylinder, $V = \pi r^2 h$, to solve problem **b**. Use 3.14 for the value of $\pi$.

**Step 3:** Use the formulas for surface area to solve problem **c**.

- Surface area of a rectangular prism:
  $SA = 2lw + 2hw + 2lh$

- Surface area of a cube: $SA = 6s^2$

- Surface area of a cylinder: $SA = 2\pi r^2 + 2\pi rh$

# GLOSSARY

**anxious**—uneasy

**area**—the amount of surface enclosed by a figure

**circumference**—the perimeter of a circle

**cube**—a solid three-dimensional figure with six congruent square faces

**cylinder**—a three-dimensional figure with two parallel and congruent regions (usually circles) joined by a curved surface

**diameter**—a line segment that goes through the center and connects two points on a circle

**essential**—absolutely necessary

**formula**—a general mathematical equation or rule

**functional**—serving a useful purpose

**net**—a two-dimensional figure that can be folded to form a solid

**radius**—a line segment extending from the center of a circle to any point on the circle

**rectangular prisms**—three-dimensional objects that have six faces that are rectangles

**square units**—units used to measure area

**storage**—a space in which to store things

**surface area**—the total area of the faces of a solid figure

**three-dimensional**—having the three dimensions: length, width, and height

**two-dimensional**—having the two dimensions: length and width

**vary**—to be different

**volume**—the amount of space occupied by a three-dimensional object

# INDEX

## Let's Explore Math

**Page 6:**

**a.** 3,822 in.³

**b.** 2 ft.

**Page 9:**

**a.** Find the number of cubes in the top layer by multiplying length by width.

**b.** 10 layers

**c.** 1,000 in.³

**d.** A cube is a rectangular prism where the length, width, and height are all the same.

**Page 11:**

**a.** Trunk of car: $V = 32.4$ ft.³; Moving truck cargo space: $V = 1,647.36$ ft.³

**b.** About 50 loads

**Page 15:**

**a.** 38.47 cm²

**b.** 384.7 cm³

**c.** 609.29 cm³

**Page 17:**

**a.** 1,470 ft.³

**b.** 138.16 ft.³

**c.** The actual volume would be less than the volume found in problem **b.**

**Page 17** (cont.):

**d.** The formulas are different because the formula for finding the volume of a rectangular prism is different from the formula for finding the volume of a cylinder.

**Page 19:**

**a.** Floor: $A = 528$ ft.²;
Floor + ceiling: $A = 1,056$ ft.²

**b.** Side wall: $A = 220$ ft.²;
Both side walls: $A = 440$ ft.²

**c.** Back wall: $A = 240$ ft.²;
Back wall + front wall: $A = 480$ ft.²

**d.** $SA = 1,056 + 440 + 480 = 1,976$ ft.²

**e.** 4 cans of paint
($SA = 1,552$ ft.²; $1,552 \div 388 = 4$)

**f.** $SA = 2lw + 2lh + 2wh$ or
$SA = 2(lw + lh + wh)$

**Page 21:**

96 m²

**Page 23:**

**a.** $A = 20.1$ ft.²

**b.** 3.14 ft.²; 6.28 ft.²

**c.** $SA = 26.38$ ft.²

**d.** $SA = 2\pi r^2 + 2\pi rh$

**Page 25:**

$SA = 116.1$ ft.²

$V = 68.9$ ft.³

## Problem-Solving Activity

**a.** All dimensions of Container B are the same. $V = 85.18$ ft.³

**b.** $V = 17.4$ ft.³

**c.** Container A: 69.82 ft.²; Container B: 116.16 ft.²; Container C: 39.54 ft.²

**d.** Volume is the most important measurement because it indicates how much space a 3-D shape occupies.